My United States

North Dakota

ANN O. SQUIRE

Children's Press®
An Imprint of Scholastic Inc.

Content Consultant
James Wolfinger, PhD, Associate Dean and Professor
College of Education, DePaul University, Chicago, Illinois

Library of Congress Cataloging-in-Publication
Names: Squire, Ann, author.
Title: North Dakota / by Ann O. Squire.
Description: New York, NY : Children's Press, Scholastic Inc., 2019. | Series: A true book | Includes bibliographical
    references and index.
Identifiers: LCCN 2017054804 | ISBN 9780531235676 (library binding) | ISBN 9780531250860 (pbk.)
Subjects: LCSH: North Dakota—Juvenile literature
Classification: LCC F636.3 .S68 2019 | DDC 978.4—dc23
LC record available at https://lccn.loc.gov/2017054804

Photographs ©: cover: Tom Bean/Alamy Images; back cover bottom: Richard Cummins/Getty Images; back cover ribbon: AliceLiddelle/
Getty Images; 3 bottom: Radharc Images/Alamy Images; 3 map: Jim McMahon/Mapman ®; 4 bottom: Dan Thornberg/Shutterstock;
4 top: Paul Starosta/Getty Images; 5 top: Dennis Macdonald/Getty Images; 5 bottom: Neal Mishler/Alamy Images; 7 top: North Wind
Picture Archives/Alamy Images; 7 bottom: Danita Delimont/Getty Images; 7 center bottom: Mark Newman/FLPA/Minden Pictures; 7
top: Jim West/age fotostock; 8-9: Tim Fitzharris/Minden Pictures; 11: Dennis Macdonald/Getty Images; 12: Daniel Barry/Getty Images;
13: Gerry Ellis/Minden Pictures; 14: John Pitcher/age fotostock; 15: GeoStock/Getty Images; 16-17: Ilene MacDonald/Alamy Images; 19:
csfotoimages/iStockphoto; 20: Tigatelu/Dreamstime; 22 right: Pakmor/Shutterstock; 22 left: Atlaspix/Shutterstock; 23 bottom right:
Neal Mishler/Alamy Images; 23 top right: Dan Thornberg/Shutterstock; 23 top left: Paul Starosta/Getty Images; 23 center left: Maksym
Bondarchuk/Shutterstock; 23 bottom left: Milos Luzanin/Shutterstock; 23 center right: Don Johnston/Getty Images; 24-25: Stocktrek
Images/Superstock, Inc.; 27: Edward Curtis/The Granger Collection; 29: Danita Delimont/Alamy Images; 30 left: French-Canadian
explorer Pierre Gaultier de Varennes, sieur de La Vérendrye (colour litho), Canadian School, (20th century) / Private Collection/Peter
Newark Pictures/Bridgeman Images; 30 right: North Wind Picture Archives/Alamy Images; 31 bottom: Historical/Corbis/Getty Images;
31 top right: Jean-Erick PASQUIER/Gamma-Rapho/Getty Images; 31 top left: Atlaspix/Shutterstock; 32: Universal History Archive/UIG/
Getty Images; 33: Allan Davey; 34-35: Michael Ochs Archives/Getty Images; 36: KeithSzafranski/iStockphoto; 37: Minot Daily News,
Nancy Kuehn/AP Images; 38: Ivan Dmitri/Michael Ochs Archives/Getty Images; 39: Andrew Burton/Getty Images; 40 inset: Rosemary
Calvert/Getty Images; 40 background: PepitoPhotos/iStockphoto; 41: Macduff Everton/Getty Images; 42 bottom left: Getty Images; 42
top right: Henry Gris/FPG/Getty Images; 42 center right: Jack Mitchell/Getty Images; 42 bottom right: Bettmann/Getty Images; 42 top
left: Pictorial Press Ltd/Alamy Images; 43 center left: Ulf Andersen/Getty Images; 43 center right: Allstar Picture Library/Alamy Images;
43 bottom right: Donald Kravitz/Dick Clark Productions/Getty Images; 43 bottom left: Jim Spellman/WireImage/Getty Images; 43 top
left: Michael Levin/Corbis/Getty Images; 44 bottom: PaulPaladin/Alamy Images; 44 top: Andre Jenny/Alamy Images; 44 center: Niday
Picture Library/Alamy Images; 45 center: Phil Schermeister/Getty Images; 45 top left: Washington Imaging/Alamy Images; 45 top right:
Andre Jenny/Alamy Images; 45 bottom: Daniel Barry/Getty Images.

Maps by Map Hero, Inc.

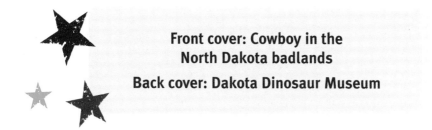

**Front cover: Cowboy in the
North Dakota badlands**

Back cover: Dakota Dinosaur Museum

Welcome to North Dakota

Key Facts

Capital: Bismarck

Estimated population as of 2017: 755,393

Nickname: Peace Garden State

Biggest cities: Fargo, Bismarck, Grand Forks

UNITED STATES

North Dakota

Find the Truth!

Everything you are about to read is true **except** for one of the sentences on this page.

Which one is **TRUE**?

T or F It rarely gets cold enough to snow in North Dakota.

T or F The country's largest flour mill is owned by the state of North Dakota.

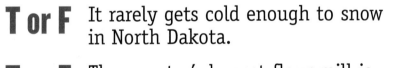

Discover the Spirit

HIP 409

NORTH DAKOTA
PEACE GARDEN STATE

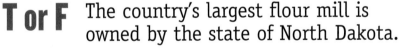

Find the answers in this book.

Contents

THE **BIG** TRUTH!

Wild
prairie rose

What Represents North Dakota?

Northern pike

4

Theodore Roosevelt
National Park

3 History

How did North Dakota become
the state it is today?

4 Culture

What do North Dakotans do for work and fun?

Western
meadowlark

5

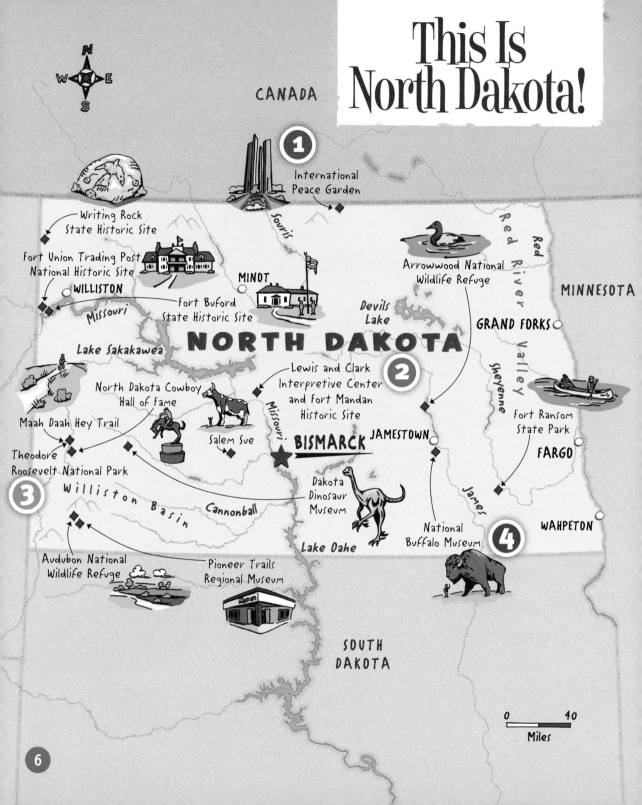

This Is North Dakota!

CANADA

1 International Peace Garden

Souris

Writing Rock State Historic Site

Fort Union Trading Post National Historic Site

WILLISTON

Fort Buford State Historic Site

MINOT

Missouri

Lake Sakakawea

Devils Lake

Arrowwood National Wildlife Refuge

Red River

MINNESOTA

GRAND FORKS

Red River Valley

NORTH DAKOTA

2

North Dakota Cowboy Hall of Fame

Lewis and Clark Interpretive Center and Fort Mandan Historic Site

Salem Sue

Maah Daah Hey Trail

Missouri

Theodore Roosevelt National Park

3

Williston Basin

Cannonball

Audubon National Wildlife Refuge

Pioneer Trails Regional Museum

Dakota Dinosaur Museum

BISMARCK

JAMESTOWN

Sheyenne

Fort Ransom State Park

FARGO

James

National Buffalo Museum

4

WAHPETON

Lake Oahe

SOUTH DAKOTA

N W E S

0   40
Miles

① International Peace Garden

Located along the U.S.-Canada border, this garden celebrates the peaceful relationship between the two nations. It features a giant floral clock, a chime of 14 bells, and a peace chapel.

② Lewis and Clark Interpretive Center

At this historic site in Washburn, visitors can learn about the Lewis and Clark expedition. Traveling from St. Louis all the way to the Pacific Ocean, Lewis and Clark spent more time in North Dakota than in any other state.

③ Theodore Roosevelt National Park

This park in western North Dakota marks the spot where the Great Plains meets the rugged badlands. It is a **habitat** for bison, elk, and many other animals.

IIGAN

④ National Buffalo Museum

Visitors to this site in Jamestown can see bison, which are considered a sacred animal by many Native American cultures. The site is even home to a rare all-white, or albino, buffalo (pictured).

North Dakota has an area of 70,698 square miles (183,107 square kilometers), making it the country's 19th-largest state.

CHAPTER 1

Land and Wildlife

North Dakota is located in the Great Plains region of the United States. It is also in the very middle of North America. A stone marker in the town of Rugby marks the geographic center of the continent. North Dakota is just south of the Canadian provinces of Saskatchewan and Manitoba. To the west is Montana, to the south is South Dakota, and to the east is Minnesota.

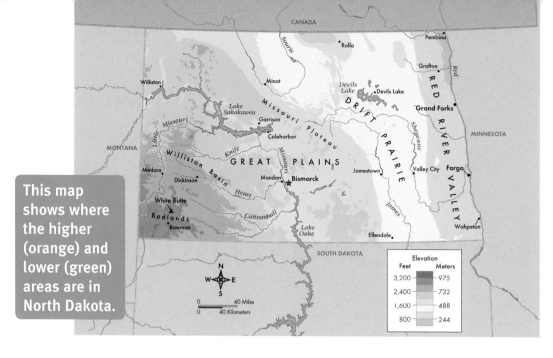

This map shows where the higher (orange) and lower (green) areas are in North Dakota.

Elevation	
Feet	Meters
3,200	975
2,400	732
1,600	488
800	244

Highs and Lows

The lowest area of North Dakota is found in the eastern part of the state, in the Red River Valley. It lies about 800 to 1,000 feet (244 to 305 meters) above sea level. Moving westward, the land begins to rise to the Drift Prairie and then the Missouri Plateau (the North Dakota portion of the Great Plains). The highest point in North Dakota is White Butte, in the southwestern region. It reaches a height of 3,506 feet (1,069 m).

The Badlands

The southwestern part of North Dakota is covered in a type of rugged land called badlands. The area features a dramatic landscape where rocks have been carved into fantastic shapes by centuries of **erosion**. A dry, rocky landscape, the North Dakota badlands provide a habitat for coyotes, snakes, bison, prairie dogs, and other desert dwellers. The Lakota people were the first to call this area *mako sica*, or "land bad," because of the rugged terrain, extreme temperatures, and lack of water.

Theodore Roosevelt National Park is located within the North Dakota badlands.

MAXIMUM TEMPERATURE
121°F

MINIMUM TEMPERATURE
-60°F

Winter storms can dump more than a foot of snow at once on cities such as Fargo.

What's the Weather?

North Dakota's **climate** changes dramatically from summer to winter. Summers are almost always hot, while winters can be brutally cold. The weather is **humid** in the eastern part of the state, but dry in the west. North Dakota's weather can be unpredictable, with snowstorms occurring almost as frequently in fall and spring as they do during the winter.

Prairies, Wetlands, and Farms

North Dakota was once covered with tallgrass, short-grass, and mixed-grass **prairies**, as well as wetland areas. People have cleared the prairies and filled in wetlands to create farmland. As a result, prairies have almost completely disappeared, and wetlands have decreased from 5 million acres (2 million hectares) to about 2.7 million acres (1.1 million ha). Today, nearly 90 percent of the state's land is used for farms and ranches.

Upper Souris National Wildlife Refuge is a large area of protected prairie land in north-central North Dakota.

North Dakota Wildlife

As many habitats have been converted to farmland, North Dakota's wildlife has been affected. Birds and reptiles have declined, as have large mammals such as mountain lions, mule deer, and bison. Another thing affecting the state's wildlife is energy development. North Dakota is one of the leading oil-producing states in the nation. When humans and oil-drilling equipment move in, native animal and plant species are pushed out.

Mountain lions are especially common in the badlands of western North Dakota.

There are more than 1,500 wind turbines in North Dakota.

Alternative Energy

The Prairie Potholes region, an area of shallow wetlands, covers a large part of northeastern North Dakota. It provides a habitat for many bird species. There are also many wind farms in this region. A renewable energy like wind power may be better for the planet than **fossil fuels**. However, the spinning blades of wind turbines can kill birds that fly past. Scientists are working to find a solution that protects birds while allowing development of this important alternative energy resource.

North Dakota's capitol stands almost 242 feet (74 m) tall.

CHAPTER 2

Government

Bismarck has been North Dakota's capital since 1889, when the state was created from the Dakota **Territory**. There have been two state capitols. The first building was completed in 1884, before North Dakota was even a state! That building burned to the ground in 1930 because of a fire that started in a janitor's closet. The new capitol is a 21-story skyscraper that houses the governor's office and many other state departments.

State Government

North Dakota's government is made up of three branches. The executive branch is headed by the governor. It is responsible for a number of state departments and agencies. The legislative branch consists of the Senate and the House of Representatives, and it makes new state laws. The judicial branch is made up of the court system.

NORTH DAKOTA'S STATE GOVERNMENT

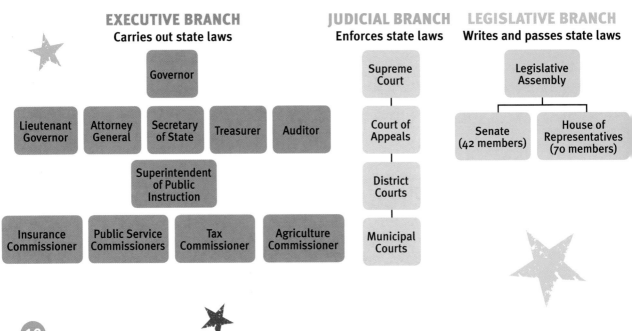

EXECUTIVE BRANCH
Carries out state laws

- Governor
- Lieutenant Governor
- Attorney General
- Secretary of State
- Treasurer
- Auditor
- Superintendent of Public Instruction
- Insurance Commissioner
- Public Service Commissioners
- Tax Commissioner
- Agriculture Commissioner

JUDICIAL BRANCH
Enforces state laws

- Supreme Court
- Court of Appeals
- District Courts
- Municipal Courts

LEGISLATIVE BRANCH
Writes and passes state laws

- Legislative Assembly
- Senate (42 members)
- House of Representatives (70 members)

The Nonpartisan League

In the early 1900s, a group of North Dakota reformers got together and asked for big changes in the state's government. The Nonpartisan League (NPL) demanded that the state take ownership of banks, grain elevators, and mills. It also wanted voting rights for women. Though the NPL did not last long, it brought changes that endure today. Both the Bank of North Dakota and the largest flour mill in the country are owned by the state.

North Dakota's National Role

Each state elects officials to represent it in the U.S. Congress. Like every state, North Dakota has two senators. The U.S. House of Representatives relies on a state's population to determine its numbers. North Dakota has just one representative in the House.

Every four years, states vote on the next U.S. president. Each state is granted a number of electoral votes based on its number of members in Congress. With two senators and one representative, North Dakota has three electoral votes.

2 senators and 1 representative

3 electoral votes

With three electoral votes, North Dakota's voice in presidential elections is below average compared to other states.

The People of North Dakota

Elected officials in North Dakota represent a population with a range of interests, lifestyles, and backgrounds.

Ethnicity (2016 estimates)

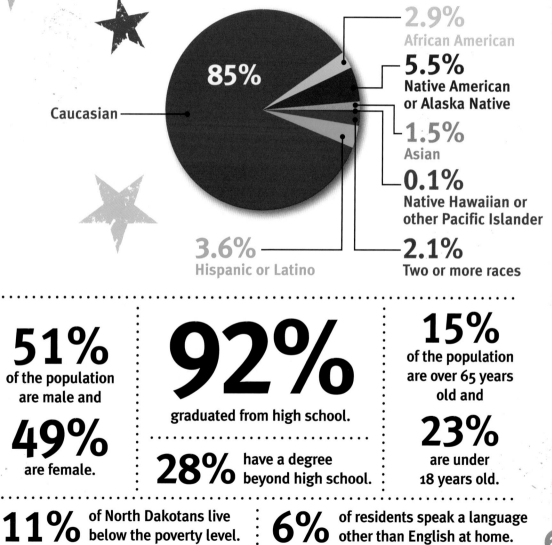

85%
Caucasian

2.9%
African American

5.5%
Native American or Alaska Native

1.5%
Asian

0.1%
Native Hawaiian or other Pacific Islander

3.6%
Hispanic or Latino

2.1%
Two or more races

51%
of the population are male and
49%
are female.

92%
graduated from high school.

28% have a degree beyond high school.

15%
of the population are over 65 years old and
23%
are under 18 years old.

11% of North Dakotans live below the poverty level.

6% of residents speak a language other than English at home.

What Represents North Dakota?

States choose specific animals, plants, and objects to represent the values and characteristics of the land and its people. Find out why these symbols were chosen to represent North Dakota or discover surprising curiosities about them.

Seal

In the center of the state seal are a number of symbols of North Dakota's history, including farming tools and a Native American on horseback hunting bison. The phrase "Liberty and Union Now and Forever One and Inseparable" appears over a field of 42 stars. The number of stars represents the 42 states that made up the United States in 1889, when North Dakota became a state.

Flag

The state flag features a bald eagle holding an olive branch and a bundle of arrows in its talons. In its beak is a ribbon that reads *E Pluribus Unum*. This is a Latin phrase meaning "out of many, one." It refers to the way each U.S. state is part of a larger country. The 13 stripes on the eagle's breast and the 13 stars above it represent the original states that made up the United States.

Wild Prairie Rose

STATE FLOWER
This bright-pink rose can be seen growing wild throughout North Dakota.

Northern Pike

STATE FISH
Fishers travel from around the world to catch huge northern pike in the waters of North Dakota.

Chokecherry

STATE FRUIT
This tasty fruit grows wild across much of North Dakota.

American Elm

STATE TREE
Common across North Dakota, this beautiful tree has green leaves that turn gold in autumn.

Convergent Lady Beetle

STATE INSECT
Ladybugs were chosen to represent the state in 2011 by a group of elementary school students.

Western Meadowlark

STATE BIRD
This yellow-and-black songbird can often be seen perched on fence posts in the state's fields and meadows.

Mammoths have been extinct since about 1650 BCE.

CHAPTER 3

History

Archaeologists believe that early humans made their way to North America by crossing a land bridge from Asia. About 15,000 years ago, these early settlers made their way to what is now North Dakota. The climate was warming, and there were large animals such as mammoths and mastodons to hunt for food. The new settlers used a type of stone called Knife River flint to make spears and other tools. As time went on, the larger animals disappeared, and early people began hunting smaller game, as well as gathering plant foods.

The Woodland Period

In about 500 BCE, some of North Dakota's Native Americans started learning skills that changed their way of life. Some planted seeds to raise sunflowers and other crops. Farming required them to stay in one place, so they began to form permanent settlements. Others kept their **nomadic** lifestyle, moving from place to place in search of bison and other game. Eventually, they began to use bows and arrows, and later horses, in their hunts.

This map shows some of the major tribes that lived in what is now North Dakota before Europeans came.

The Nakota and other Sioux people traveled often and lived in tipis, which were easy to set up and take down as needed.

A Range of Cultures

Over time, several Native American cultures developed in North Dakota. Among them were the Assiniboine, the Chippewa, the Hidatsa, the Mandan, and the Arikara.

In the 1600s, the Dakota Sioux people arrived in the area from the east. They continued spreading out into North Dakota's plains and eventually split into three main groups: the Dakota, the Nakota, and the Lakota. Together, they are known as the Sioux Nation.

Exploring North Dakota

In 1738, a Canadian explorer named Pierre Gaultier de La Vérendrye led a group of explorers down into North Dakota. At first, Europeans were not very interested in this vast, difficult land. But in the late 1700s, the demand for animal furs brought traders to the area. By 1803, the United States owned the land that is now North Dakota, having purchased the enormous Louisiana Territory from France.

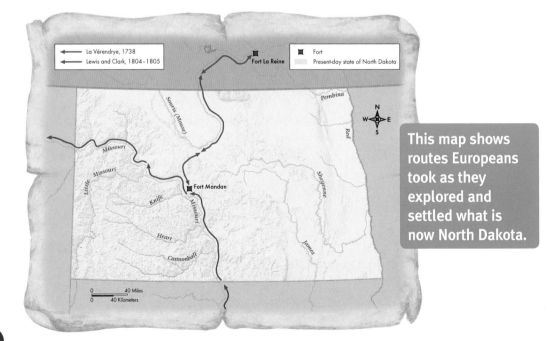

La Vérendrye, 1738
Lewis and Clark, 1804–1805

Fort La Reine

Fort
Present-day state of North Dakota

Souris (Mouse)

Pembina

Red

Missouri

Little Missouri

Knife

Fort Mandan

Missouri

Sheyenne

Heart

Cannonball

James

0   40 Miles
0   40 Kilometers

This map shows routes Europeans took as they explored and settled what is now North Dakota.

The Lewis and Clark Expedition

In 1804, President Thomas Jefferson sent two explorers, Meriwether Lewis and William Clark, to explore the Louisiana Territory. They spent a great deal of time in what is now North Dakota, meeting many Native American groups along the way. Lewis and Clark built Fort Mandan near present-day Washburn and waited out the first winter of their journey there. It was here that the explorers met a Native American woman named Sacagawea, who served as their interpreter and guide.

Settling the Prairie

The fur trade grew quickly, and by the early 1800s there was a permanent European settlement in North Dakota's Red River Valley. More settlers arrived, and hunters killed thousands of bison. In 1874, gold was discovered in what is now South Dakota. This led to more settlers in the area and more conflicts with Native Americans, who were eventually forced onto **reservations**.

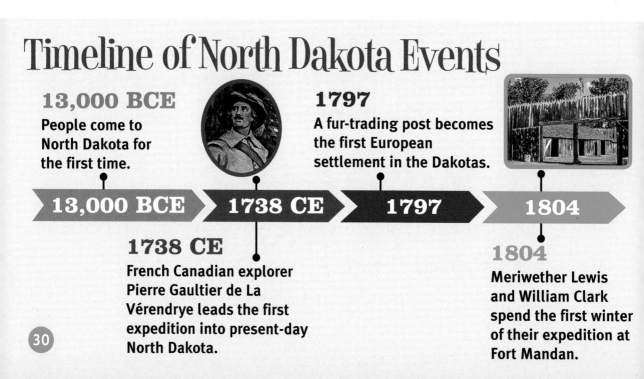

Timeline of North Dakota Events

13,000 BCE
People come to North Dakota for the first time.

1797
A fur-trading post becomes the first European settlement in the Dakotas.

| 13,000 BCE | 1738 CE | 1797 | 1804 |

1738 CE
French Canadian explorer Pierre Gaultier de La Vérendrye leads the first expedition into present-day North Dakota.

1804
Meriwether Lewis and William Clark spend the first winter of their expedition at Fort Mandan.

Farms and Ranches

As railroads opened up the Dakota Territory, settlers flooded in from northern European countries such as Norway, Sweden, and Germany, as well as from Canada and the eastern part of the United States. The land and climate were perfect for growing wheat, and soon eastern North Dakota boasted many large farms. Farther west, ranchers brought cattle to graze on the rich grasslands.

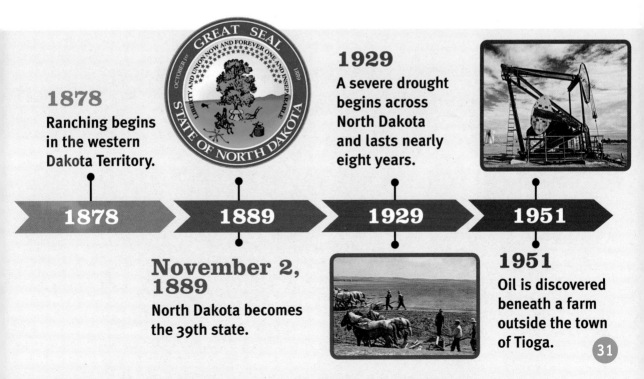

1878
Ranching begins in the western Dakota Territory.

1929
A severe drought begins across North Dakota and lasts nearly eight years.

1878   **1889**   **1929**   **1951**

November 2, 1889
North Dakota becomes the 39th state.

1951
Oil is discovered beneath a farm outside the town of Tioga.

From Territory to State

By the late 1800s, several hundred thousand people lived in the Dakota Territory. They wanted statehood. In 1889, President Benjamin Harrison signed a bill admitting North and South Dakota to the United States as two separate states.

In the 1930s, a severe drought in North Dakota put many farmers out of business. In the 1950s, oil was discovered in northwestern North Dakota, providing an economic boost.

Many of North Dakota's farming families left the state during the drought of the 1930s.

Sacagawea

Sacagawea was a Shoshone woman who met Lewis and Clark in North Dakota and accompanied them on their expedition to explore the western part of North America. Born in Idaho, she had been brought to North Dakota by a Canadian fur trapper named Toussaint Charbonneau. She had a good knowledge of the area and of native plants. In addition, she spoke several languages.

At one point, the explorers encountered a group of Shoshone. They hoped to trade with the Shoshone to get horses and supplies for their travels toward the Pacific Ocean. It turned out that the Shoshone chief was Sacagawea's older brother, and she hadn't seen him for many years. The Shoshone helped Lewis and Clark, sending them on their way with horses and guides.

The Assiniboine are also known as the Nakota.

A group of Assiniboine men plays drums at a 1963 gathering in the city of Bismarck.

CHAPTER 4

Culture

Today, the cultural life of North Dakota is still strongly influenced by the area's earliest residents. Native American beadwork, pottery, and other crafts can be seen throughout the state. Another big influence on North Dakota comes from the many northern European immigrants who settled in the region. Norwegian, Danish, Icelandic, and German traditions—including foods, celebrations, and even languages—are a big part of the state's unique culture.

Sports and Recreation

Fishing, hiking, and hunting are favorite activities. In the winter, North Dakotans turn to snowmobiling and ice fishing. Basketball is popular, and North Dakotans are proud that Phil Jackson, one of the most successful coaches in the history of pro basketball, played at the University of North

Dakota. Baseball also has an important history in the state. North Dakota teams were racially **integrated** long before those of the major leagues. And Roger Maris, one of the most famous baseball players of all time, grew up in Fargo.

To go ice fishing, people drill holes in thick, sturdy ice and lower their lines into the freezing water below.

Traditional Norwegian dancers perform at Norsk Høstfest in Minot.

Celebrations From Around the World

North Dakota's Native American, Scandinavian, and German heritages come through in many of the state's festivals. The United Tribes International Powwow in Bismarck draws Native American dancers and drummers representing more than 70 tribes. The annual Norsk Høstfest in Minot is the largest Scandinavian festival in the country. It celebrates everything Danish, Norwegian, Swedish, Finnish, and Icelandic. North Dakota's German residents are not left out. Several cities host a yearly Oktoberfest, featuring German food, music, and other traditions.

About 19,200 farms in North Dakota grow wheat, making it one of the state's top crops.

North Dakota's Economy

Agriculture is big business in North Dakota. About one in four North Dakotans works in farming or ranching. The state is the largest producer in the country of many cereal grains. It also produces flax, sunflower seeds, and beans. Energy is another big part of North Dakota's economy. The state has both oil and coal reserves. Renewable wind energy has become big business in North Dakota. Tourism is the state's third-largest business, bringing in more than $3 billion every year.

A Changing State

North Dakota's economy and jobs have long depended on the land. For years, agriculture was the biggest business. Then the discovery of huge oil reserves made energy an important source of jobs and income. But depending so heavily on these two areas has caused problems for the state. When demand for oil is high, North Dakota's economy booms. But when there is plenty of oil to go around and prices drop, there are fewer jobs and less income for North Dakotans. The same is true for agriculture. Many experts believe that bringing different types of business into the state is needed to give North Dakota's people a more reliable source of jobs and money.

A worker lines up a pipe for drilling oil at a facility near Watford City.

North Dakota Cuisine

North Dakota's best-known foods can be traced back to the state's northern European settlers. Ukrainian cheese buttons, lefse (a type of thin potato pancake from Norway), and lutefisk (a dried cod dish eaten in Sweden and Norway) are all favorites in North Dakota today.

★ Sunflower Seed Cookies

Ask an adult to help you!

North Dakota grows more sunflowers than any other state. Here's a tasty way to use the seeds!

Ingredients

$\frac{1}{3}$ cup all-purpose flour
$\frac{1}{2}$ teaspoon baking soda
$\frac{1}{2}$ teaspoon salt
$\frac{1}{3}$ cup unsalted butter, softened
$\frac{1}{3}$ cup granulated sugar
1 small egg

1 teaspoon vanilla extract
$\frac{1}{2}$ cup quick-cooking oats
$\frac{1}{3}$ cup roasted, unsalted sunflower seeds
$\frac{1}{2}$ cup raisins
$\frac{1}{4}$ cup chocolate chips

Directions

Preheat the oven to 350 degrees. In a small bowl, combine flour, baking soda and salt. In a large bowl, beat the butter and sugar together. Beat in the egg and vanilla extract. Add the flour mixture and beat until combined. Stir in the remaining ingredients. Drop by spoonfuls, 2 inches apart, onto nonstick baking sheets. Bake for 12 to 14 minutes. Remove and set the cookies on wire racks to cool.

Horseback riders enjoy the scenery at Theodore Roosevelt National Park.

Something for Everyone

Whether you're interested in history, outdoor adventures, Native American culture, wildlife, or dramatic scenery, North Dakota is a great place to take it all in. Powwows and other events will give you a good sense of this state's original inhabitants. A visit to one of the state's many wildlife refuges will let you view amazing animals. From the rugged badlands to cities like Bismarck, there's something for everyone in North Dakota. ★

Famous People

Sitting Bull

(ca. 1831–1890) was a Dakota leader who resisted the attempts of the U.S. government to force Native Americans onto reservations. He was born and spent most of his life in the Dakota Territory.

Angie Dickinson

(1931–) is an Emmy and Golden Globe award–winning actress. She was born in Kulm, where her father was publisher of the local newspaper.

James Rosenquist

(1933–2017) was an artist well known for his pop art paintings. He was from Grand Forks.

Peggy Lee

(1920–2002) was a singer, songwriter, composer, and actress whose career lasted for 60 years. She was born in Jamestown.

Roger Maris

(1934–1985) was a famous baseball player who broke Babe Ruth's home-run record. He grew up in Fargo.

Bobby Vee

(1943–2016) was a rock 'n' roll and pop singer who was a teen idol in the 1960s. He was born in Fargo.

Josh Duhamel ★

(1972–) is an actor who is well known for his work in the *Transformers* films. He was born in Minot.

Louise Erdrich

(1954–) is a noted Chippewa author of novels, poetry, and children's books. She grew up in Wahpeton, where her parents taught at a Bureau of Indian Affairs school.

Cara Mund

(1993–) was crowned Miss America 2018. She is a Bismarck native.

Christopher Michael Holley

(1971–) is an actor who has appeared in such films as *Smokin' Aces* and *21*. He is from Minot.

Did You Know That ...

The world's largest scrap metal sculptures can be found along the 32-mile long (51-kilometer) Enchanted Highway in southwestern North Dakota.

North Dakota grows more sunflowers than any other state. And 2016 was a record year. North Dakota farms produced 1.14 billion pounds (517 million kilograms) of sunflowers.

Huge herds of bison once roamed the North Dakota plains. By 1900, they had been hunted nearly to extinction. President Theodore Roosevelt spearheaded efforts to save them, and today tens of thousands of bison live in the North Dakota grasslands.

About 25 billion tons of coal lie just under the surface of western North Dakota. That's enough to supply the region's energy needs for 800 years.

Salem Sue, a giant sculpture of a Holstein cow, is 38 feet (12 m) high and 50 feet (15 m) long, and is made of 6 tons of reinforced fiberglass. Standing on a hill in New Salem, Sue can be seen from many miles away.

With an average of only 17 inches (43 centimeters) of precipitation each year, North Dakota is one of the driest states in the country.

Did you find the truth?

F It rarely gets cold enough to snow in North Dakota.

T The country's largest flour mill is owned by the state of North Dakota.

Resources

Books

Englar, Mary. *The Great Plains Indians: Daily Life in the 1700s*. North Mankato, MN: Capstone Press, 2005.

Kamma, Anne. *If You Were a Pioneer on the Prairie*. New York: Scholastic Paperbacks, 2003.

Rozett, Louise (ed.). *Fast Facts About the 50 States: Plus Puerto Rico and Washington, D.C.* New York: Children's Press, 2010.

Stille, Darlene R. *North Dakota*. New York: Children's Press, 2015.

Visit this Scholastic website for more information on North Dakota:

★ www.factsfornow.scholastic.com
Enter the keywords **North Dakota**

Important Words

agriculture (AG-rih-kuhl-chur) the raising of crops and animals

climate (KLYE-mit) the weather typical of a place over a long period of time

erosion (ih-ROH-zhuhn) the process of wearing away gradually by water or wind

fossil fuels (FAH-suhl FYOO-uhlz) coal, oil, or natural gas, formed from the remains of prehistoric plants and animals

habitat (HAB-ih-tat) the place where a plant or animal is usually found

humid (HYOO-mid) describing weather that is moist and usually very warm, in a way that is uncomfortable

integrated (IN-tuh-gray-tid) not separated by race; open to or used by all sorts of people

nomadic (noh-MAD-ik) describing members of a community that travels from place to place instead of living in the same place all the time

prairies (PRAIR-eez) large areas of flat or rolling grassland with few or no trees

reservations (rez-ur-VAY-shuhnz) areas of land set aside by the government for Native American people

territory (TER-ih-tor-ee) an area connected with or owned by a country that is outside the country's main borders

Index

Page numbers in **bold** indicate illustrations.

About the Author

Ann O. Squire is a psychologist and an animal behaviorist. Before becoming a writer, she studied the behavior of rats, tropical fish in the Caribbean, and electric fish from central Africa. Her favorite part of being a writer is the chance to learn as much as she can about all sorts of topics. In addition to *North Dakota*, Dr. Squire has written books about several other states as well as health, earth science, planets, weather, and many types of animals. She lives in Asheville, North Carolina.